IN THE BEGINNING
THE FIRST SEVEN DAYS

WRITTEN BY DAVIS CARMAN
ILLUSTRATED BY ANDERSON CARMAN

IN THE BEGINNING

Published by
Apologia Educational Ministries, Inc.
1106 Meridian Plaza, Suite 220/340
Anderson, Indiana 46016
apologia.com

Manufactured in the USA
Printed by Bang Printing, Brainerd, MN
First Printing: March 2015

ISBN: 978-1-940110-67-7

Book Design: Doug Powell
Illustrations: Anderson Carman

This book is dedicated to Anderson Carman.
I enjoyed working on this project with you, son.
May you shine brightly for God's glory in all of your artistic endeavors.

INTRODUCTION

This book was written to help your children learn, live, and defend the Christian faith. The words and illustrations are a biblical account of what happened during the first seven days of creation. For example, after God created man and woman, He gave them five things to do. This book depicts their duties in a way that will make the message clear for children and instill in them a desire to know God and humbly pursue His will for their lives.

Of course, for us to learn anything about God, He must reveal Himself to us. God does this in two primary ways. One way is through His Word, the Bible. A second way is through His creation. Let's take a closer look at these two ways your children can come to know our God.

GOD REVEALED IN HIS WORD

The first book of the Bible is Genesis, a word that means "beginning." Genesis is a record of history from the very beginning, when space, time, and matter were created out of nothing. Indeed, this is the original book of origins.

The Bible is the very word of God. He inspired forty men over 1,500 years to write down His truths as a way to reveal Himself to mankind. Romans 10:17 says that faith comes from hearing, and hearing by the word of God. The Gospel of John tells us that God's Word is truth and that it sanctifies us, which is the progress of becoming holy and righteous (John 17:17). John also recorded one of the most famous and wondrous statements of all time: "For God so loved the world that he gave his one and only Son, that whoever believes in him shall not perish but have eternal life" (John 3:16).

It is important that our children read and hear God's Word in order to understand His will for them, experience His grace, and build the kind of faith in Jesus Christ that saves.

GOD REVEALED IN CREATION

"The heavens declare the glory of God; the skies proclaim the work of his hands" (Psalm 19:1). Creation speaks loud and clear. Therefore people are without excuse when it comes to knowing that God exists (Romans 1:20). Observing nature will lead your children to see that the created works of God are amazing, complex, and have a purpose.

Through the centuries, as scientists have used the scientific method to test their ideas and theories, two things remain clear: Creation had a beginning, and there is so much yet to explore and discover. From the vastness of space and its billions of galaxies to the tiniest of electrons swirling around unseen to form the building blocks of matter, it's clear that there is a Creator, and He is God Almighty.

LEARNING BY DOING

A good way to reinforce any learning is through simple activities. Here are some suggestions for helping your children to learn the seven days of creation and what they have to teach us. Don't try to do everything. Let this be a pleasant, non-stressful time to build on your relationship with your children. Observe how they process the words of God and watch them fall in love with their Creator.

BEFORE THE WORLD BEGAN

Read John 1 and discuss how Jesus existed before the world was formed.

Ask them what it might have been like when time did not exist.

DAY ONE

Discuss why we are often scared in a dark room.

Discuss why turning on a light allows us to see things better.

Read John 1:4–5, John 3:19–21, and John 8:12 and discuss what it means that Jesus is the light of the world.

Read Matthew 6:22–23 and discuss why we need to have God's light inside us.

3

DAY TWO

Locate, identify, and draw some clouds (for example, cirrus, cumulonimbus, stratus).
Take the air temperature every morning, afternoon, and evening for a week.
Put up a windsock or flag outdoors and track the wind direction once a day for a week.
Use a rain gauge to measure the rainfall for a month.

DAY THREE

Collect some rocks and identify them.
Collect or draw some tree leaves and identify them.
Collect some flowers and press them in a book.
Plant a bean seed and watch it germinate.

DAY FOUR

Watch a sunrise and locate which direction is east.
Watch a sunset and locate which direction is west.
Track the phases of the moon for a month.
Locate and identify the Little Dipper in the night sky.
Discuss how there are twenty-four hours in a day based on the Earth's rotation about its axis.
Explain how God established the seven-day week.
Explain how we know when spring, summer, fall, and winter begin.
Explain that there are 365 days in a year based on the Earth's revolving around the sun.

DAY FIVE

Draw a fish, whale, shark, octopus, or other swimming creatures.
Draw a robin, eagle, owl, heron, or other flying creatures.

DAY SIX

Draw a cow, horse, dog, cat, or other domesticated animals.
Draw a lion, tiger, elephant, rhino, buffalo, deer, or other wild animals.
Draw a snake, lizard, beetle, spider, ant, or other creeping animals.
Draw a man and woman working together to make something.
Draw a man and woman getting married or taking care of a baby.
Draw a man and woman taking care of animals or the earth.

DAY SEVEN

Take time to rest and think about God, Jesus, the Holy Spirit, and heaven.
Write a short letter to God praising Him for making all of creation.
Take a nap.

I hope and pray that this book will increase the knowledge, wisdom, and courage in your children to help them grow from young disciples of Jesus into mature Christians, ready to defend the reasons for the hope that lies within them (1 Peter 3:15).

Now turn the page and read what happened . . . in the beginning.

Davis

DAVIS CARMAN

4

BEFORE THE WORLD BEGAN

ONLY GOD EXISTED. HE EXISTED AS FATHER, SON, AND HOLY SPIRIT.

NOTHING ELSE EXISTED.

EVEN TIME DID NOT EXIST.

IN THE BEGINNING, GOD CREATED
THE HEAVENS AND THE EARTH.

THE SPIRIT OF GOD HOVERED OVER THE WATERS.

THEN GOD SAID, "LET THERE BE LIGHT."
AND THERE WAS LIGHT.

GOD SEPARATED THE LIGHT

HE CALLED THE LIGHT "DAY"

AND CALLED THE
DARKNESS "NIGHT."

THERE WAS EVENING, AND THERE WAS MORNING. AND THAT WAS THE FIRST DAY.

GOD SAID, "LET THERE BE AN EXPANSE TO SEPARATE WATER FROM WATER."

AND THERE APPEARED A SPACE BETWEEN THE WATERS
OF THE HEAVENS FROM THE WATERS OF THE EARTH.

GOD CALLED THE EXPANSE "SKY."

THERE WAS EVENING, AND THERE WAS MORNING.
AND THAT WAS THE SECOND DAY.

GOD THEN GATHERED THE WATER UNDER THE SKY TO FLOW INTO ONE PLACE SO THAT DRY GROUND APPEARED.

HE CALLED THE DRY GROUND "LAND."

HE CALLED THE WATERS "SEAS."

AND STREAMS CAME UP FROM THE EARTH AND
WATERED THE WHOLE SURFACE OF THE LAND.

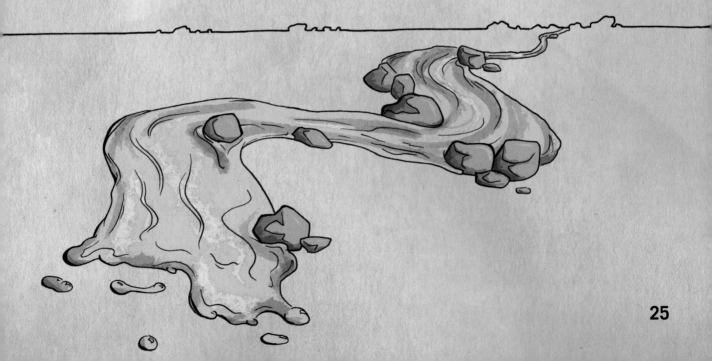

THEN GOD SAID, "LET THE LAND PRODUCE VEGETATION."

ALL SORTS OF PLANTS AND
TREES GREW, AND THEIR SEEDS
PRODUCED MORE PLANTS AND
TREES OF THE SAME KIND.

AND GOD SAW THAT IT WAS GOOD.

THERE WAS EVENING, AND THERE WAS MORNING.
AND THAT WAS THE THIRD DAY.

THEN GOD CREATED THE SUN,
THE MOON, AND THE STARS.

THEY SEPARATED THE DAY FROM THE NIGHT.

AND THEY WOULD BE SIGNS TO MARK
THE SEASONS, DAYS, AND YEARS.

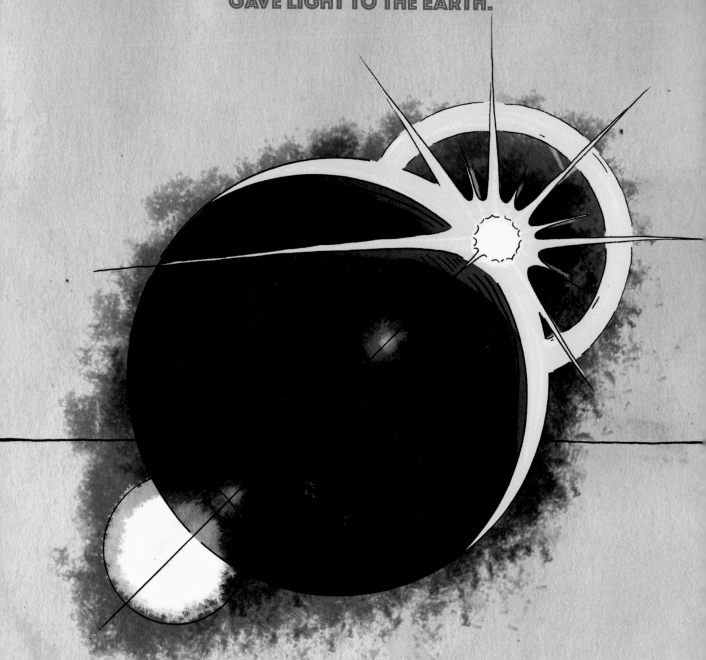

THE SUN, MOON, AND STARS
GAVE LIGHT TO THE EARTH.

AND GOD SAW THAT IT WAS GOOD.

THERE WAS EVENING, AND THERE WAS MORNING.
AND THAT WAS THE FOURTH DAY.

AND HE FILLED THE SKY WITH FLYING CREATURES.

HE BLESSED THEM AND SAID, "BE
FRUITFUL AND MULTIPLY."

AND GOD SAW THAT IT WAS GOOD.

THERE WAS EVENING, AND THERE WAS MORNING. AND THAT WAS THE FIFTH DAY.

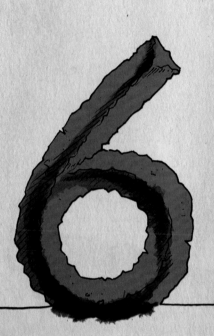

GOD SAID, "LET THE LAND PRODUCE LIVING ANIMALS."

HE MADE DOMESTICATED ANIMALS.

AND WILD ANIMALS.

AND CREEPING ANIMALS THAT
MOVE ALONG THE GROUND.

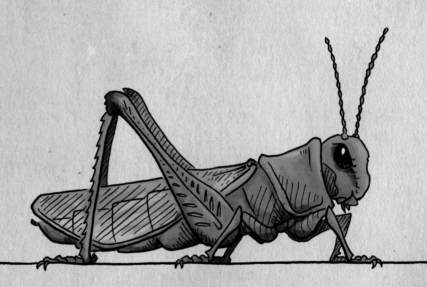

AND GOD SAW THAT IT WAS GOOD.

THEN GOD SAID, "LET US MAKE MANKIND IN OUR IMAGE, IN OUR LIKENESS, AND LET THEM RULE OVER ALL THE EARTH."

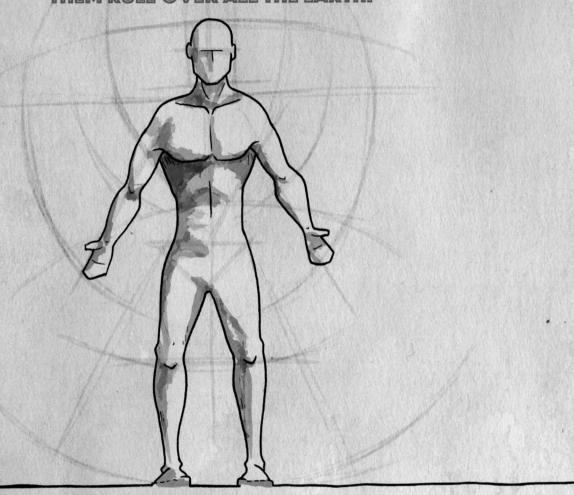

AND SO HE FORMED A MAN FROM THE
DUST OF THE GROUND.

GOD BREATHED INTO HIS NOSTRILS THE BREATHE
OF LIFE, AND THE MAN BECAME A LIVING BEING.

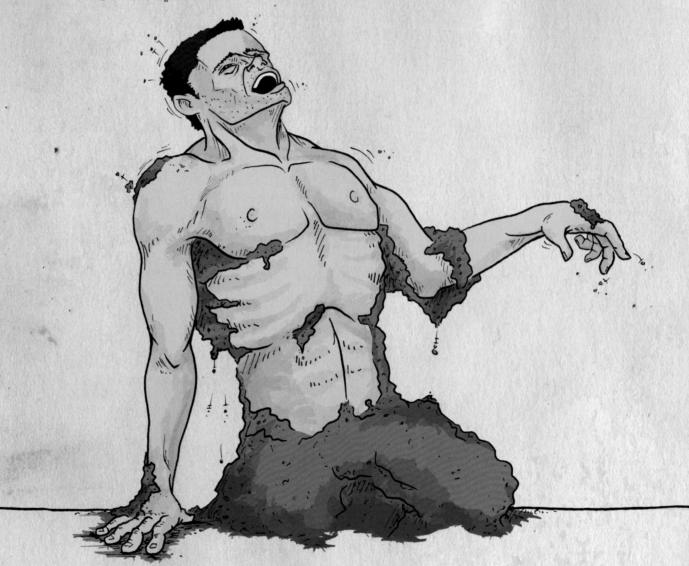

THEN GOD PLANTED A GARDEN IN THE EAST, IN EDEN.
HE TOOK THE MAN AND PLACED HIM THERE TO WORK
THE GARDEN AND TAKE CARE OF IT.

A RIVER WATERED THE GARDEN.
IN THE MIDDLE OF THE GARDEN OF EDEN WERE TWO TREES.

GOD TOLD THE MAN, "YOU ARE FREE TO
EAT FROM ANY TREE IN THE GARDEN."

BUT YOU MUST NOT EAT FROM THE TREE OF THE KNOWLEDGE OF GOOD AND EVIL.

THEN GOD SAID, "IT IS NOT GOOD FOR THE MAN TO BE ALONE. I WILL MAKE A HELPER SUITABLE FOR HIM."

GOD BROUGHT THE BIRDS AND LIVESTOCK AND WILD ANIMALS TO THE MAN, AND THE MAN GAVE NAMES TO ALL THE CREATURES.

BUT NONE WAS A SUITABLE HELPER FOR HIM.

SO GOD CAUSED THE MAN TO FALL INTO A DEEP SLEEP,
AND HE MADE A WOMAN FROM ONE OF THE MAN'S RIBS.

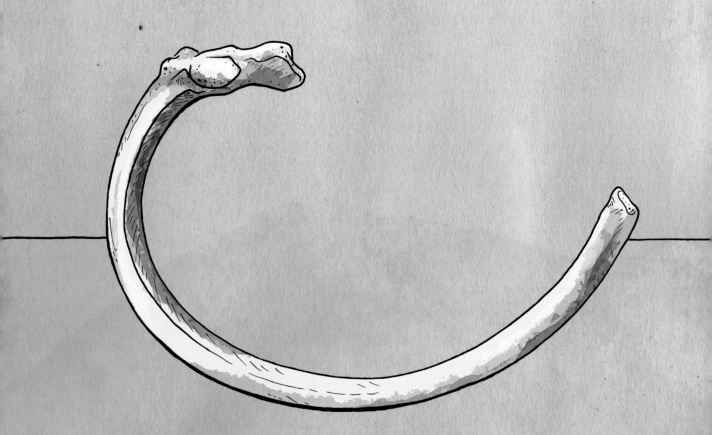

THUS GOD CREATED MALE AND FEMALE.

THE MAN AND WOMAN WERE UNITED AS HUSBAND
AND WIFE, AND THEY BECAME ONE FLESH.

AND GOD GAVE THE MAN AND
WOMAN FIVE THINGS TO DO.

GOD TOLD THEM TO BE FRUITFUL AND PROSPER.

GOD TOLD THEM TO HAVE CHILDREN AND
INCREASE IN NUMBER.

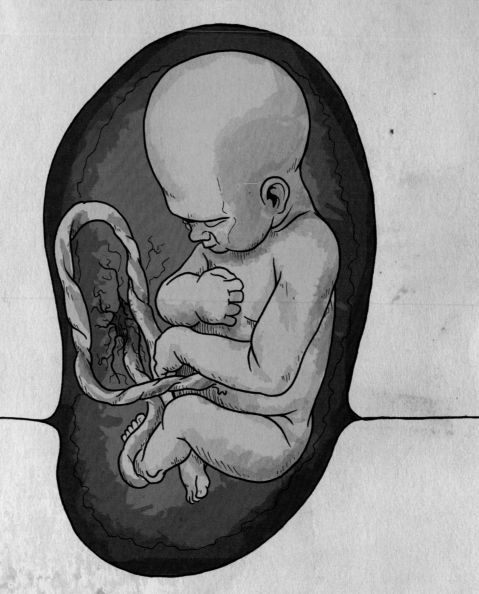

GOD TOLD THEM TO FILL THE EARTH.

GOD TOLD THEM TO TAKE CHARGE OF THE EARTH AND USE ITS RESOURCES TO SERVE GOD AND MAN.

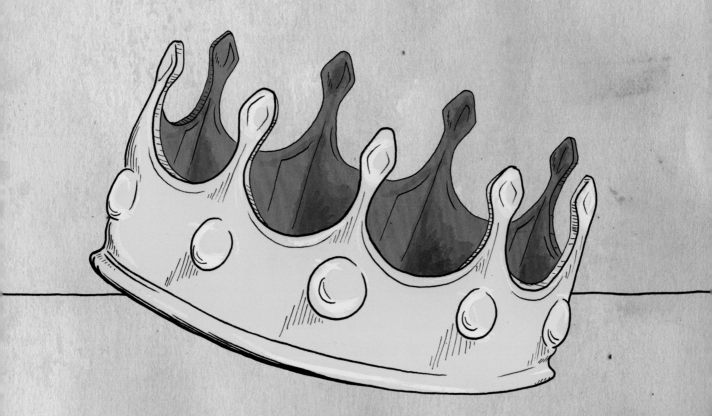

GOD TOLD THEM TO RULE OVER EVERY
LIVING CREATURE AND CARE FOR THEM.

GOD SAW EVERYTHING HE HAD MADE,
AND IT WAS VERY GOOD.

THERE WAS EVENING, AND THERE WAS MORNING.
AND THAT WAS THE SIXTH DAY.

GOD RESTED FROM HIS WORK.

HE BLESSED THE SEVENTH DAY AND MADE IT HOLY.

WE ARE TO REMEMBER THE SABBATH DAY BY KEEPING IT HOLY.

THE EARTH IS THE LORD'S, AND EVERYTHING IN
IT, THE WORLD, AND ALL WHO LIVE IN IT.
PSALM 24:1

ALSO BY DAVIS CARMAN

Good Morning, God
A Light for My Path